COLLINS·LONGMAN

Mapstart

Simon Catling

Principal Lecturer in Education, Oxford Polytechnic

Contents

Looking down at the ground

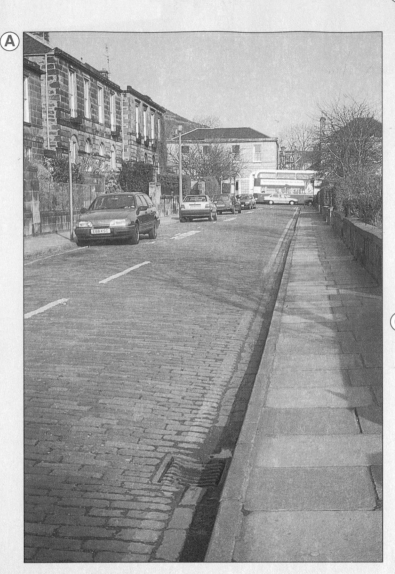

You can often see **shapes** looking down at the ground.
Look at the shapes in photo **A**.

Photos **B** and **C** show other shapes you can see looking down.

Look at the objects in photos **D**, **G** and **J**.
You can take a photo to show the **shape** of each object **looking straight down**.
You can make rubbings that show the shapes.
You can draw the shapes too.

1 Name three objects you can see in photo **B**.
2 Draw the shape of two of the objects in
3 What shape is the manhole cover in **H**?
4 What shape are the bricks in **J**?
5 Name something you have seen looking down at a path or road.
6 Make a rubbing or drawing of something you see looking down at the ground.

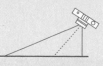

oto looking down   **A rubbing**   **A drawing**

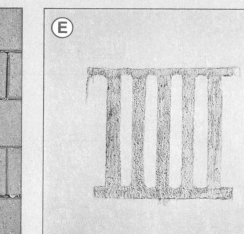

grating

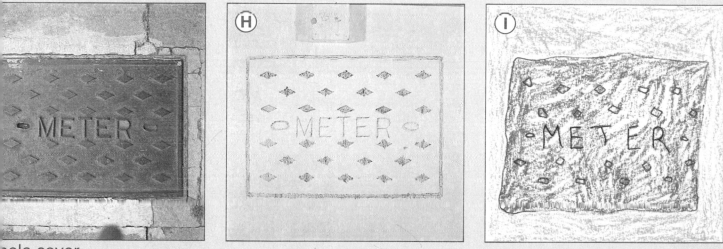

ole cover

pavement

Looking down at furniture

In photo **A** you can see inside a model house.
The house has two floors.
There is a ground floor and a first floor.

In each room you can see furniture.
Find the kitchen on the ground floor.
Find the bedroom on the first floor.

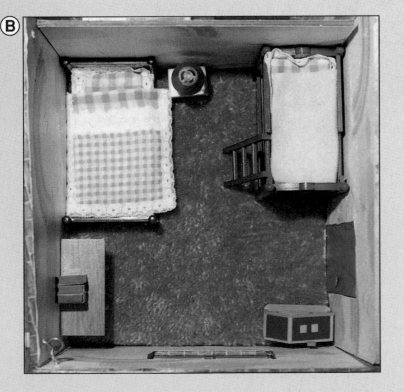

In photo **B** you are **looking straight down** into the bedroom.
You can see the shape of the room and the shape of each piece of furniture.

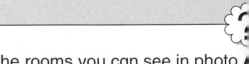

1 Name the rooms you can see in photo A of the model house.
2 Is the sitting room on the ground floor or the first floor?
3 Which floor is the bathroom on?
4 Look at photos **A** and **B**. Name the pieces of furniture you can see in the bedroom.

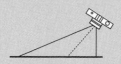

...hoto looking down

A photo looking straight down

A plan

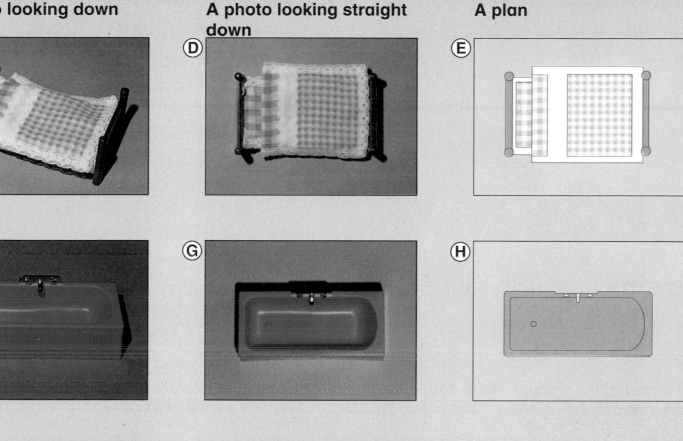

Ⓓ Ⓔ

Ⓖ Ⓗ

Ⓙ Ⓚ

...st of drawers

...for the bed in photos **A** and **B**.
...can see the same bed in photo **C**.
...oto **D** you are looking down on the bed.
...can see its shape.
...a drawing of the bed looking down from
...e.
...a **plan** of the bed.
...plan shows the shape of the bed looking
...n from above.

1 Which photo looks down from above on the bath?
2 What does the plan in **K** show?
3 Choose another piece of furniture you can see in photo **B**.
  Draw a plan of it.
4 Choose a piece of furniture in the sitting room in photo **A**.
  Draw a plan of it.

Looking down at a classroom

A

B

Pot plant

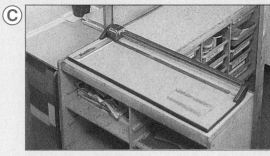

C

Paper cutter

D

Globe

A is a photo of a classroom.
You can see most of the room,
but not all of it.

Look at the furniture in the room.
See what the furniture is used for.
What else can you see in the room?

1 How many tables can you see in **A**?
2 Look at the object in photo **B**. Find it in
   What is it on?
3 Look at **C**. Find the paper cutter in **A**.
   Name something next to it.
4 Look at **D**. Where is it in the room?

MUSIC AREA

PENCIL/ CRAYON AREA

MATHS/ COMPUTER AREA

ART AREA

SHOP AREA

WORK MOUNTING AREA

READING AREA

CRAFT AREA

F

G

H

you can see the whole of the classroom.
the parts of the room you can see in **A**.
at what is in the areas you could not see.

ows you **what** is in the classroom and
re things are in the room.

a **map** of the classroom.
E uses pictures to show what is in the
.

e parts of the room have been named.

at the rubbish bin in **F**.
ows it looking down from straight above.
a plan of the bin.

1 Find the rubbish bin in **E**.
   Name something it is next to.
2 Name two parts of the classroom you can
   see in photo **A** and map **E**.
3 Name a part of the room you cannot see
   in photo **A**.
4 Where are the books kept in the
   classroom?
5 How many tables are there in the
   classroom?
6 Draw a plan of one of the tables.
7 Draw a plan of the paper cutter in **C**.

Looking down at an area

Ⓐ

Cottage · Cottage Path · Upper Bridge · Beech Tree Path · Toilets · Adventure Castle · Castle Path · Butterfly House · Butterfly Path · Garden Centre · Stream · West Path · Green Path · Green Path · Middle Drive · Middle Bridge · Art Gallery · Gallery Path · House Path · Manor House · Middle Drive · Gallery Path · Shop Path · Bridge Path · Toilets · Shop · Gate House · Arch Drive · Orange Path · Car Park · Picnic Area · Toilets · Main Gate · South Path · Tea Room · South Pa...

In **A** you can see the grounds of Manor Park.
You are looking down on the Park.
A is a **map** of Manor Park.
It shows the layout of the Park.

In the Park there are many places to see.
These places have been named in **A**.

Find Manor House.
It is in the **middle** of the Park.
There is an arch **in front** of the House.
The Boating Pond is to the **right** of the House.

Pictures **B**, **C** and **D** show three places
you can see in the Park.
Find them in **A**.

8

p

Boathouse

Toilets
Play Path
Boathouse
Play Area
Fir Tree Path
Pond Path
East Path
East Gate

Play Area

1 Look at **B**. Find it in map **A**.
   Which place is the Shop next to?
2 Look at **C**. Use **A** to help you.
   What is the place behind the Boathouse?
3 Is the Garden Centre to the left or
   the right of Manor House?
4 Name one path which leads to North Gate.
5 What is next to the Adventure Castle?
6 Which gate is the place in **D** near?
7 Name a path that is straight.

9

Looking down at a model

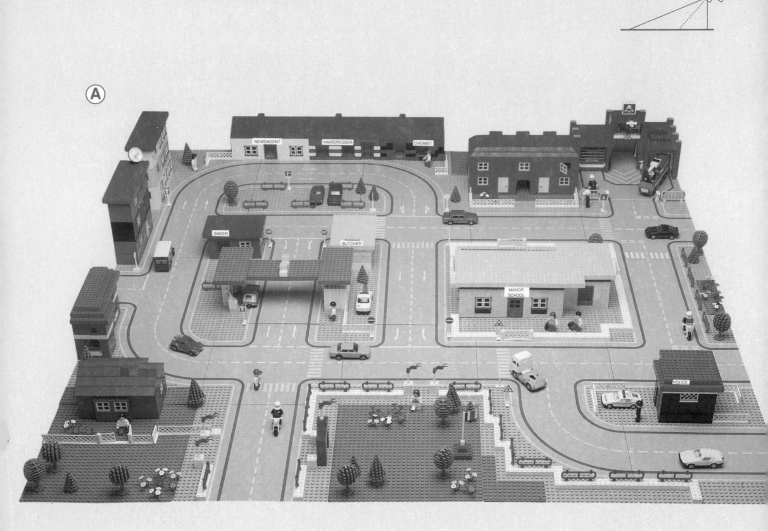

A

Labels visible on the model: NEWSAGENT, HAIRDRESSER, CHEMIST, BAKER, BUTCHER, MANOR SCHOOL, POLICE

Look at photo **A**.
You can see a model of some streets and
 buildings.
You are looking down at them from the side.
The model shows part of a town.
Look carefully to see what sort of buildings
there are.
There is a Police Station.
A police car is parked next to it.

1 Name three buildings you can see.
2 How many cars and lorries can you see
3 How many trees are there?
4 Find the breakdown truck. Is it on the
 left or the right of the garage?
5 What else can you see in photo **A**?

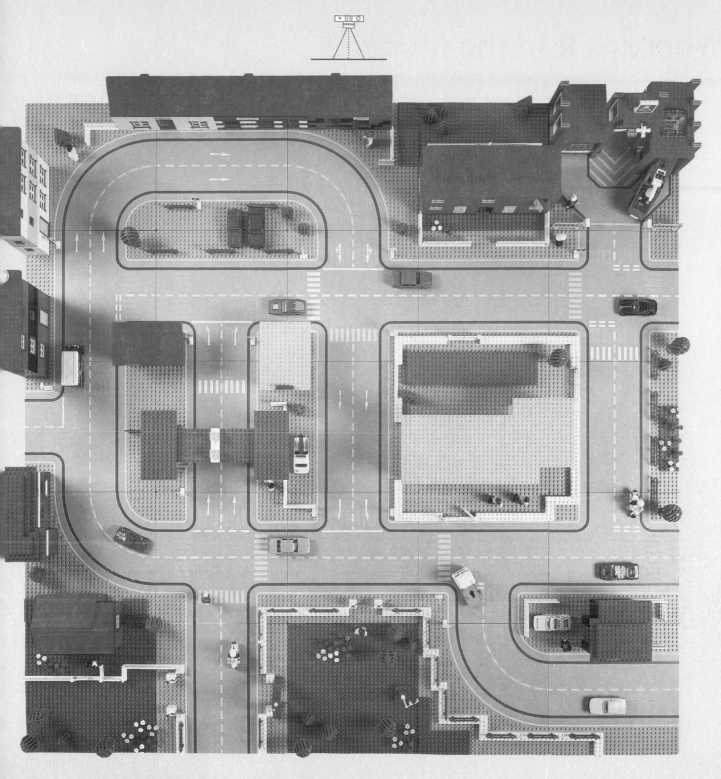

(D)

(E)

to **B** shows the model you can see in
to **A**.

are looking straight down on the model.
find the buildings and streets you can see
oto **A**.

1 Find **C**, **D** and **E** in photo **B**.
  Say what they are.
2 How many cars and lorries can you see?
3 Find the Police Station. Is there a car
  next to it going along the road?
4 Why could you not see the car in **A**?

Where is it in the model ?

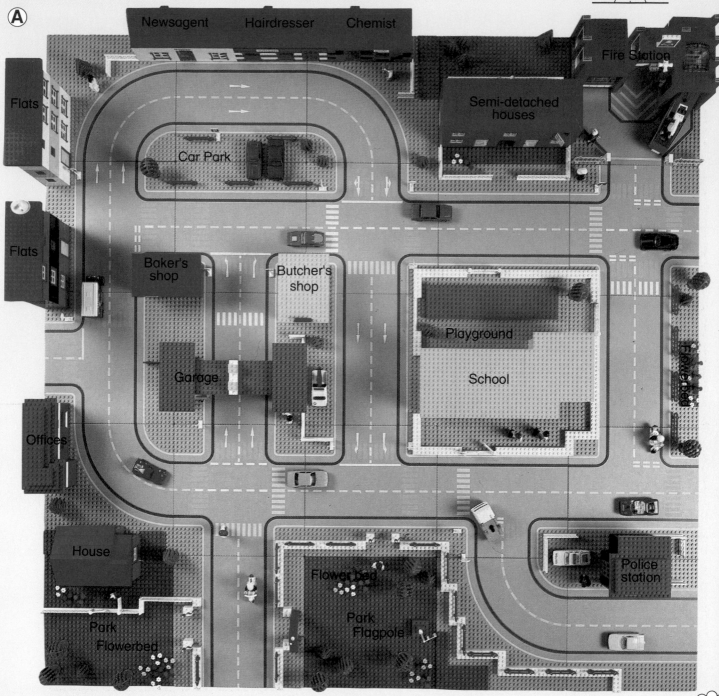

A

Newsagent   Hairdresser   Chemist

Fire Station

Flats

Semi-detached houses

Car Park

Flats

Baker's shop

Butcher's shop

Playground

Garage

School

Offices

Flowerbed

House

Flower bed

Police station

Park Flowerbed

Park Flagpole

Look at photo **A** of the model.
Some of the places have been named.
Find the places that are named.

Where is the Baker's shop?
It is **next** to the Garage.

Find the Park.
It is **beside** London Road.

1 Which building is next to the House?
2 Name the building beside the Butcher's shop.
3 What is **opposite** the Hairdresser?
4 What is on the **right** of the Semi-detached houses
5 Name something **in front** of the Fire Station.
6 Which building is **between** the Police Station
   and the Butcher's shop?

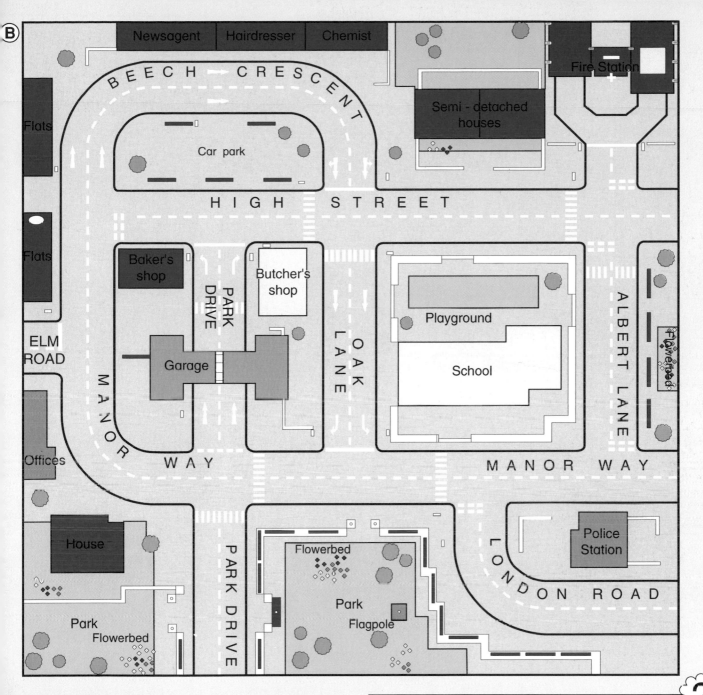

B

Newsagent | Hairdresser | Chemist

BEECH CRESCENT

Fire Station

Flats

Car park

Semi - detached houses

HIGH STREET

Flats

Baker's shop

PARK DRIVE

Butcher's shop

OAK LANE

Playground

ALBERT LANE

Flowerbed

ELM ROAD

Garage

School

MANOR WAY

Offices

MANOR WAY

House

Police Station

Park Flowerbed

PARK DRIVE

Flowerbed

Park Flagpole

LONDON ROAD

a **map** of the model.

as drawn looking down from above at the
...el. It shows the shapes of all the places in
...model.

...es plans to show what is in the model.

...ows where the places are in the
...el. The places are named on the map.
... roads are named on the map.
... maps have names on them.

1 Has the map been drawn looking from the side or looking straight down?
2 What is the shape of the Baker's shop?
3 Name three things you can see in photo **A** which are **not** in map **B**.
4 Name the building furthest away from the Fire Station in map **B**.

13

Where is it in the local area?

The front of the School

The Paddling pool

The Shops

A is a photo of Tuckswood School.
You are looking down at it.
It was taken looking down from an aeroplane.
You can see the back of the School.

B is a photo of the front of the School.
It was taken from The Green in front of the
School.
You can see trees and a lamppost in **B**.
Find them at the front of the School in photo **A**.

1 Was photo **A** taken looking down
from the side or from straight above?
2 Name three things you can see on The
Green in front of the School in photo **A**.
3 Is the Paddling pool in photo **C** at the
front or the back of the School?
4 **D** shows the Post Office. Find it in **A**.
What is between the Post Office and
the School?

14

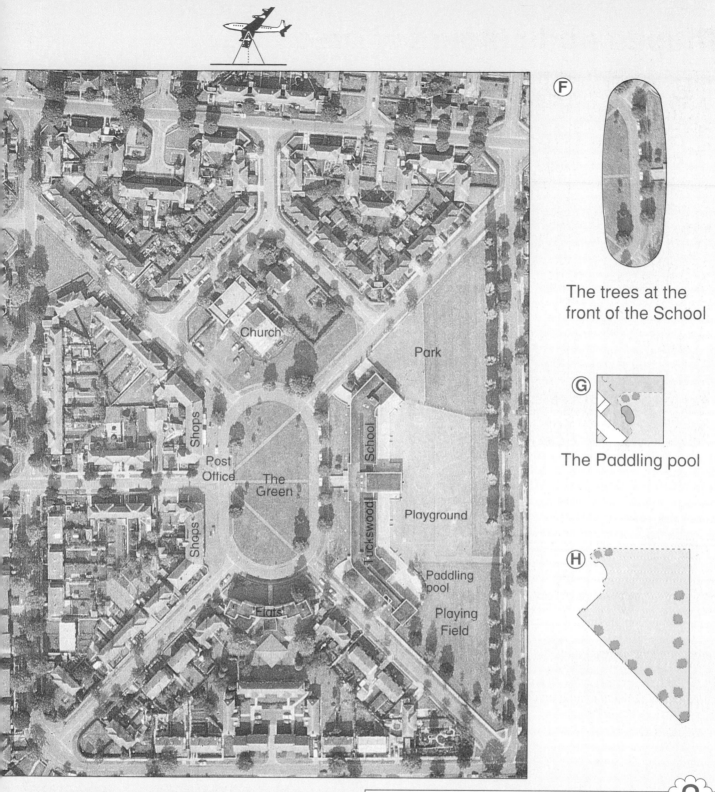

Church

Park

Shops

School

Post Office

The Green

Tuckswood

Playground

Shops

Paddling pool

Flats

Playing Field

The trees at the front of the School

The Paddling pool

a photo of the same School.
s taken looking straight down from an
plane. You can see the shape of the
ool looking down from straight above.
e of the places have been named.

to **F** shows the trees at the front of the
ool. **G** is a plan of the Paddling pool.
it in photo **E**.

1 Which part of the School does plan **H** show?
2 Draw a plan of The Green. On it show the paths and the trees.
3 What is between the Church and Playing field?
4 Draw the plan of a place far from the Park. Name it.

15

Shapes and colours

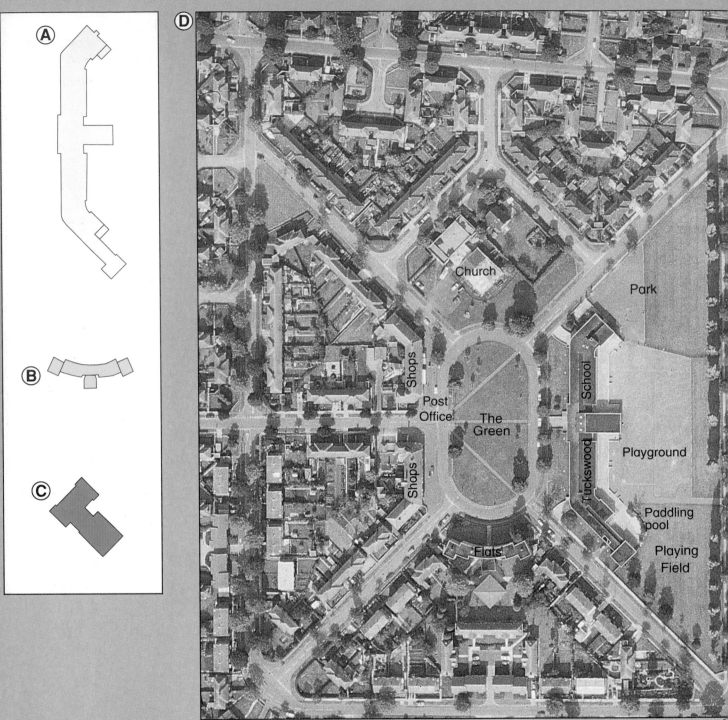

Ⓐ

Ⓑ

Ⓒ

Ⓓ

Church

Park

Shops

Post
Office

The
Green

School

Tuckswood

Playground

Shops

Paddling
pool

Flats

Playing
Field

Look carefully at photo **D**. It shows Tuckswood
School. You can see the **shapes** and **colours**
of many things. Look at the shapes of the
buildings, trees and roads.
See how many colours you can find.
Some of the places have been named.

A, **B** and **C** are plans of places you can see in
photo **D**.

1 Which building is shown in plan **A**?
2 What does plan **B** show?
3 Find and name what is shown in plan **C**
4 Draw a plan of the Park. Colour it.
5 Draw a plan of one row of Shops.
    Colour it.

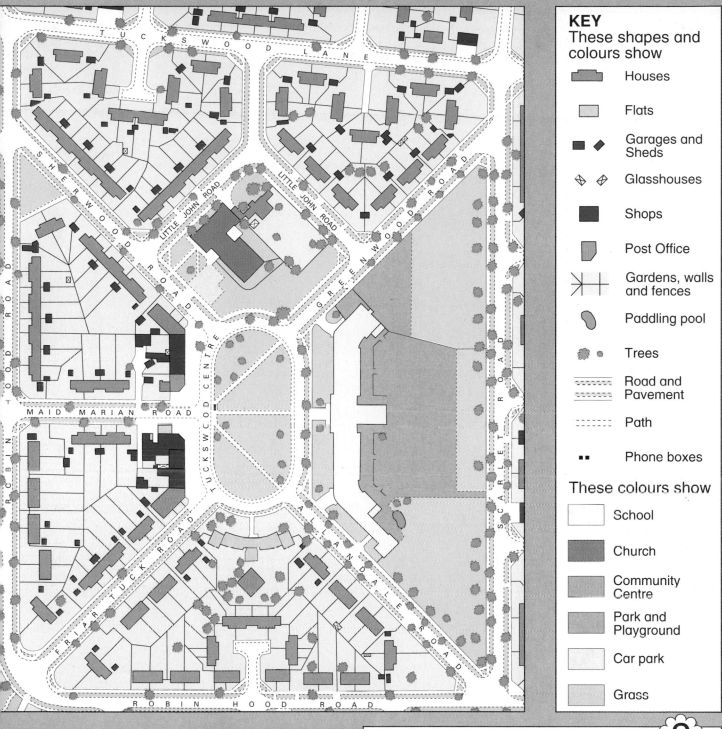

KEY
These shapes and
colours show

	Houses
	Flats
	Garages and Sheds
	Glasshouses
	Shops
	Post Office
	Gardens, walls and fences
	Paddling pool
	Trees
	Road and Pavement
	Path
	Phone boxes

These colours show

	School
	Church
	Community Centre
	Park and Playground
	Car park
	Grass

a map of the area you can see in photo **D**.
as made by tracing over the photo.

shapes and colours on the map show
erent places.

shapes and colours are named in the box
t to map **E**. This is called the **key**.

key shows what the shapes and colours
n on the map.

map **E** only the roads have been named.

1 Which colour shows the School Playground?
2 Draw the shape used to show trees.
3 Which colour shows the School building?
4 What is shown by the blue shape?
5 How are walls and fences shown in the key?
6 Why is it useful to have the roads named?

Large and small

Photo **A** shows the model town.
Some of the buildings have been named.

Find the garage in **A**.
Look at the **size** of the cars and lorries
in photo **A**.

In photo **B** you can see three cars.
They are in front of the garage.
The three cars in **B** are different sizes.
Two of the cars can drive under the
garage roof but one of them cannot.

1 What is the colour of the smallest car?
2 Which car cannot drive under the garage roof?
3 Why can it not drive under?
4 Which car do you think is the best size to go in the model?
5 Why do you think it is the best size?

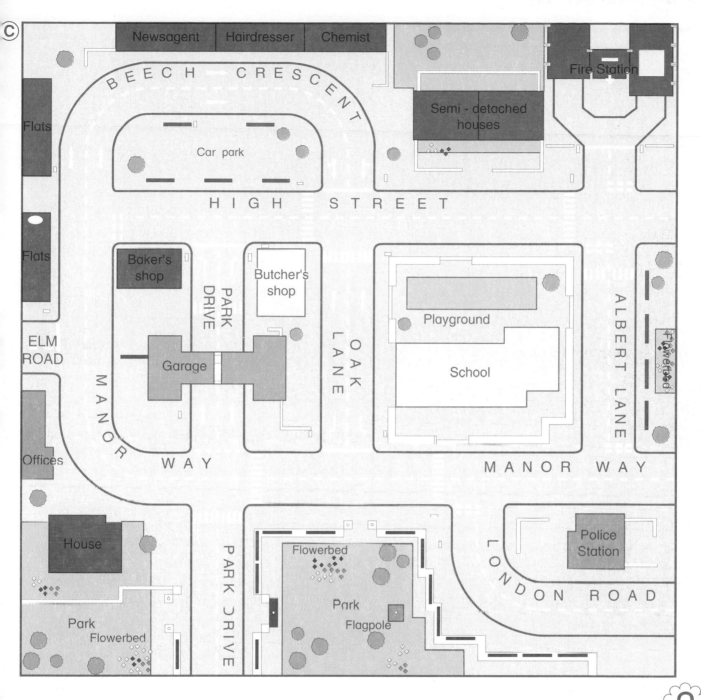

©

Newsagent | Hairdresser | Chemist

BEECH CRESCENT

Flats

Car park

HIGH STREET

Fire Station

Semi - detached houses

Flats

Baker's shop

PARK DRIVE

Butcher's shop

OAK LANE

Playground

School

ALBERT LANE

Flowerbed

ELM ROAD

Garage

MANOR WAY

MANOR WAY

Offices

LONDON ROAD

Police Station

House

PARK DRIVE

Flowerbed

Park

Flagpole

Park
Flowerbed

ⱼ at map **C** of the model.

▌ the plan of the Fire Station on map **C**.

▪lan shows how much ground it covers.

▪ows the **size** of the Fire Station.

ⱼ at the plans of other buildings.

y are different sizes.

⁣e take up a lot of space on the ground.

ⱼ at the lengths of the roads and buildings.

⁣e roads are longer than others.

⁣e roads are the same length.

1 Which is the smallest shop?
2 Is the Police Station larger or smaller than the Fire Station?
3 Does the School, the Garage or the Offices cover the most ground?
4 Which is the longest road?
5 Name two roads which are the same length.

19

Near and far

Ⓐ

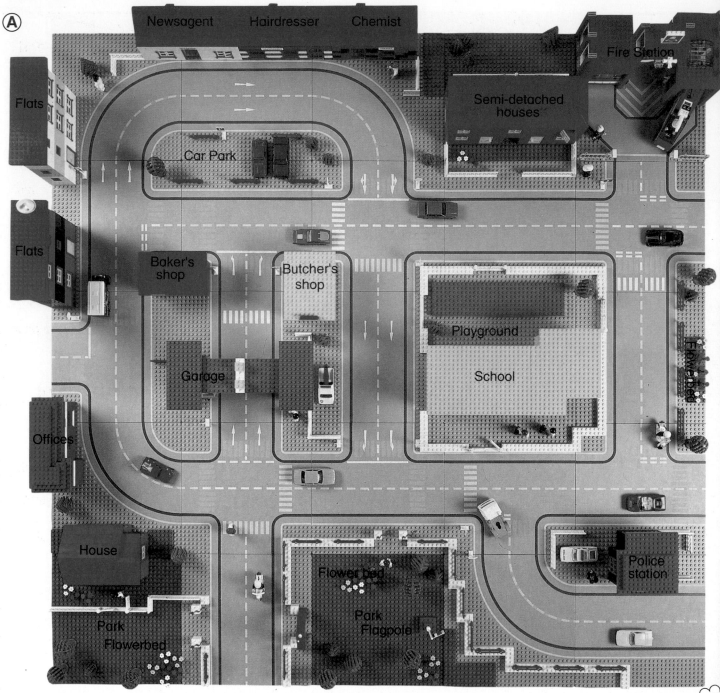

Look at photo **A** of the model. Places in it have been named.

It shows which places are **close** to each other. Find the Newsagent. One block of Flats is **near** it.

It shows places which are **far apart** from each other. The Police Station is **far away** from the Newsagent.

1 Name a shop near the Car Park.
2 Name two buildings far away from the Park.
3 Which building is **nearest** to the House
4 Is the School or the Baker's Shop **near** the Hairdresser?
5 Is the Butcher's Shop or the Chemist **furthest** from the Police Station?

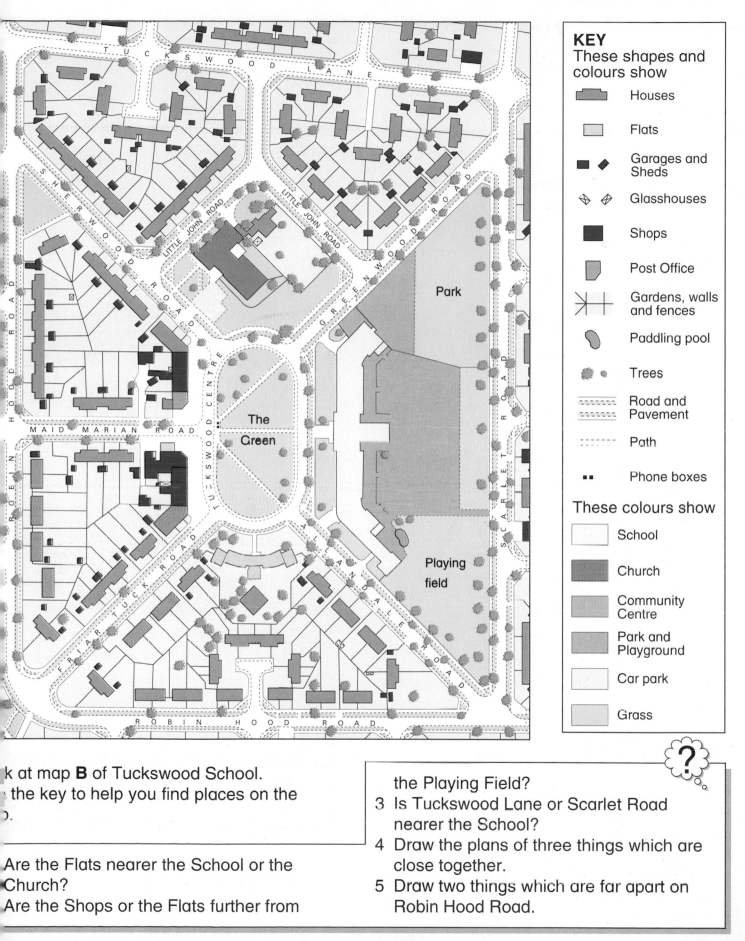

KEY

These shapes and colours show

	Houses
	Flats
	Garages and Sheds
	Glasshouses
	Shops
	Post Office
	Gardens, walls and fences
	Paddling pool
	Trees
	Road and Pavement
	Path
	Phone boxes

These colours show

	School
	Church
	Community Centre
	Park and Playground
	Car park
	Grass

Park

Playing field

The Green

...k at map **B** of Tuckswood School.
... the key to help you find places on the
...

...Are the Flats nearer the School or the
...Church?

...Are the Shops or the Flats further from

the Playing Field?

3 Is Tuckswood Lane or Scarlet Road nearer the School?

4 Draw the plans of three things which are close together.

5 Draw two things which are far apart on Robin Hood Road.

21

Which way in the model ?

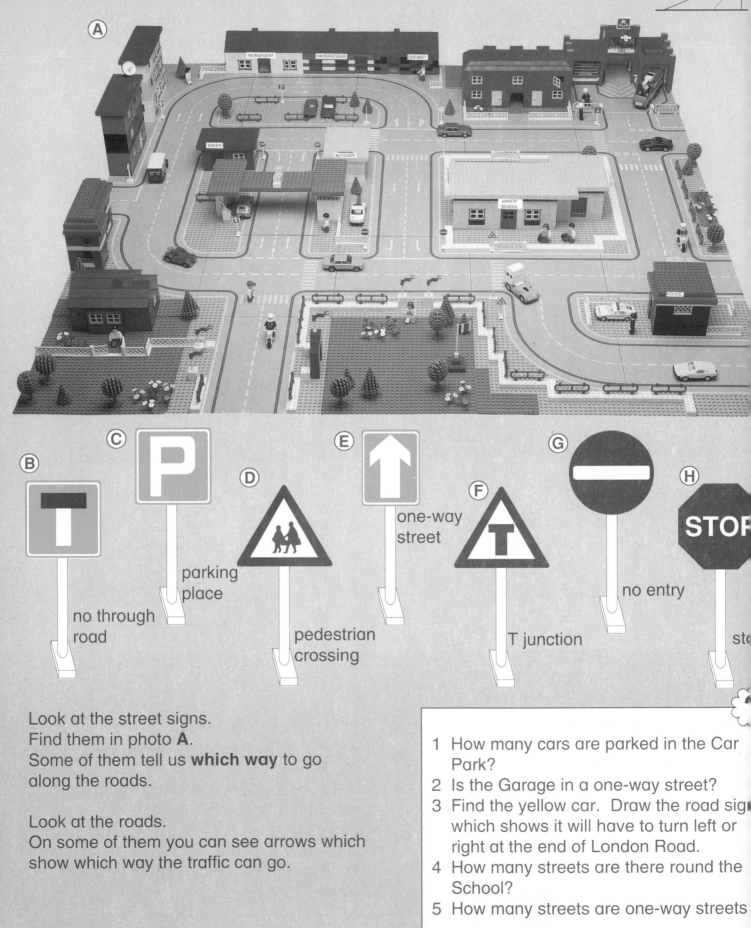

A

B no through road

C parking place

D pedestrian crossing

E one-way street

F T junction

G no entry

H STOP stop

Look at the street signs.
Find them in photo **A**.
Some of them tell us **which way** to go along the roads.

Look at the roads.
On some of them you can see arrows which show which way the traffic can go.

1 How many cars are parked in the Car Park?
2 Is the Garage in a one-way street?
3 Find the yellow car. Draw the road sign which shows it will have to turn left or right at the end of London Road.
4 How many streets are there round the School?
5 How many streets are one-way streets

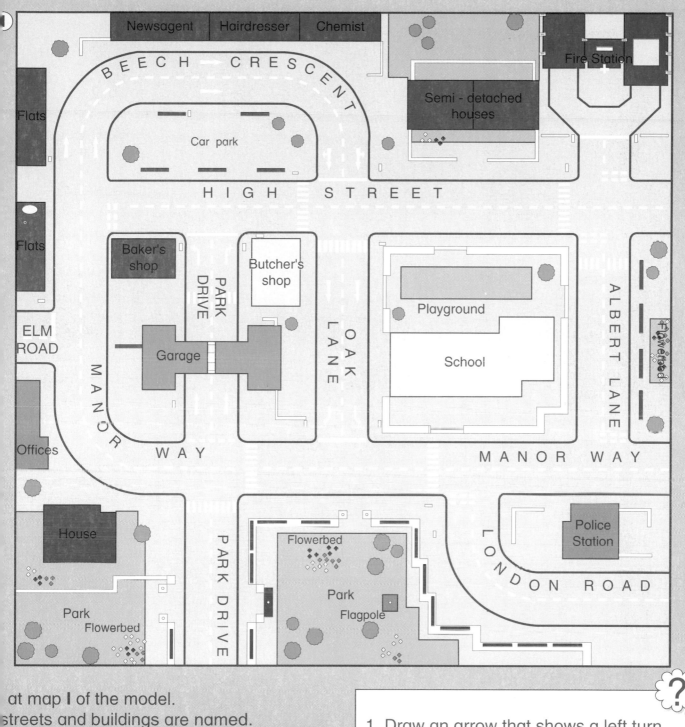

at map **I** of the model.
streets and buildings are named.
for the arrows drawn on the roads.
the Newsagent.
your finger to trace the best way along the
s from the Newsagent to the
e Station.

1 Draw an arrow that shows a left turn.
2 Name a road you cannot turn into from Manor Way.
3 Name the roads you would drive along to go from the Fire Station to the Offices.
4 To drive to the Police Station from Oak Lane, do you turn left or right into Manor Way?

Looking at the way to School

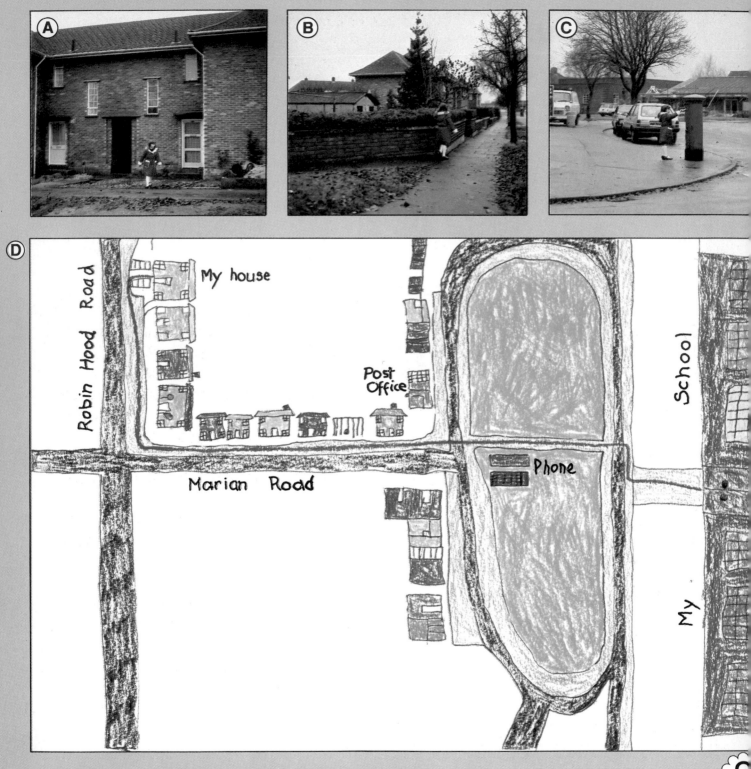

Each morning Donna walks from home to School. Photos **A**, **B** and **C** show her walking to School.

Donna has drawn a **map** of the way she walks from home to School. You can see it in **D**. She has drawn her map from memory. She shows some of the places she walks past.

1 Which way does Donna turn when she leaves home?
2 Name three places Donna walks past.
3 Is the place in photo **B** nearer the Sch○ or Donna's home?

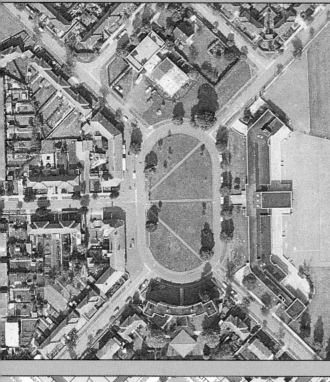

Donna goes to Tuckswood School.
Look at photo **E** and map **F**.
The map was made by tracing over the photo.
The photo and the map show Donna's home
and the School.

The way Donna walks to School is marked by
a red line. It shows her **route**.
Follow it with your finger, from her home
to the School.

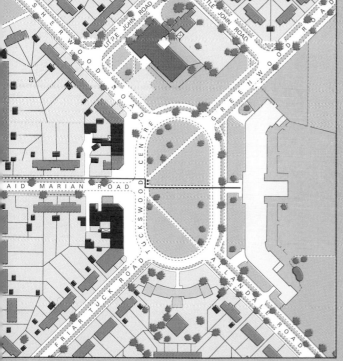

1 How many times does Donna turn
   left on her route to School?
2 Donna walks back the same way.
   How many right turns does she make?
3 Find something Donna put in the wrong
   place on her map. What Is It?
4 Donna has not drawn the postbox in
   photo **C** on her map. What should she
   draw it next to in map **D**?
5 Look at the way Donna drew her home,
   and the way it is drawn in map **F**. Which
   one shows Donna's home looking
   straight down from above?
6 Which roads does Donna walk along on
   her route from home to School.
7 Is the way Donna goes the shortest route
   from her home to the School?
8 Draw the way you go to school.

se shapes and colours show

Homes

Garages and
Sheds

Shops

Gardens, walls
and fences

Paddling pool

Trees

Road and
Pavement

Path

Donna's route

Phone boxes

These colours show

School

Church

Grass

Park and
Playground

Car park

Looking at different routes

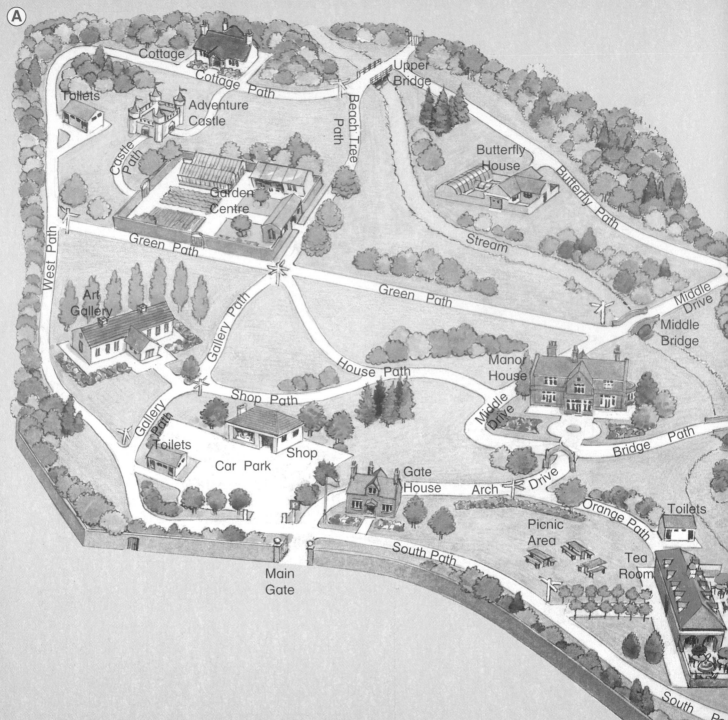

You have arrived in the Car Park for a visit to Manor Park.
You are given the picture map in **A** to help you find your way around.

The Park is a large area.
There are many places you can visit.
Find some places you would like to visit.

Pictures **B**, **C** and **D** show some places whi you might visit.
Find them in the Park.

BUTTERFLY HOUSE

© C

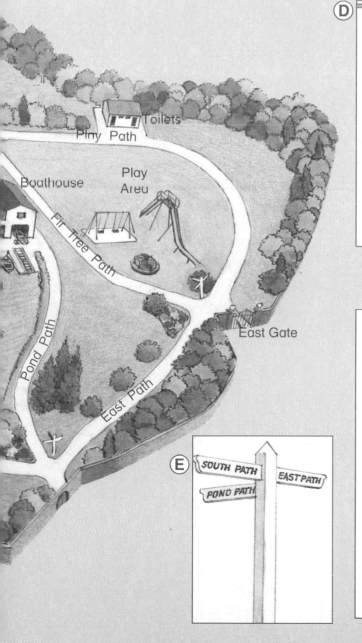

Toilets
Play Path
Play Area
Boathouse
Fir Tree Path
Pond Path
East Path
East Gate

D D

House plants

Garden Equipment

Fruit

Shrubs

Shop and office

Vegetables

Flowers

E E

SOUTH PATH
EAST PATH
POND PATH

1 Name the places in **B**, **C** and **D**.
2 Which path would you go along to get from the Car Park to Manor House?
3 You want to visit **B**. Name the paths you would go along from Manor House.
4 You are at **C**. Which paths would you walk along to get to **D**?
5 Look at **E**. Find where the three paths meet on map **A**. Is the sign post nearest the Play Area or the Boating Pond?
6 You want to go from the sign post in **E** to the Adventure Castle. Which paths would you walk along to get there?

Looking down from space at the British Isles

Satellite photo of the British Isles

Photos can be taken looking straight down from a plane.
Photos can also be taken looking at the Ea[rth] from a satellite in space.
Photo **A** shows the British Isles.
It was taken from a satellite.

The British Isles are a group of islands.
An island is a piece of land which has wate[r] all round it.
Ireland and Britain are the two largest islan[ds]

B is a map of the British Isles. It was made [by] tracing round the land in photo **A**.
Ireland and Britain are named on the map.

1. What colour is the sea in photo **A**?
2. Which colour shows the sea in Map **B**?
3. Is Ireland larger or smaller than Britain?
4. Look at photo **C**. Is the area it shows i[n] Ireland or Britain?
5. Map **D** shows some islands. Find them in **A** and **B**. Are they nearer the coast o[f] Ireland or Britain?
6. Look at the area in photo **E**. Which of t[he] two largest islands is it in?
7. **F** shows a small island. Find it in map [B] Is it near the coast of Ireland or Britain?

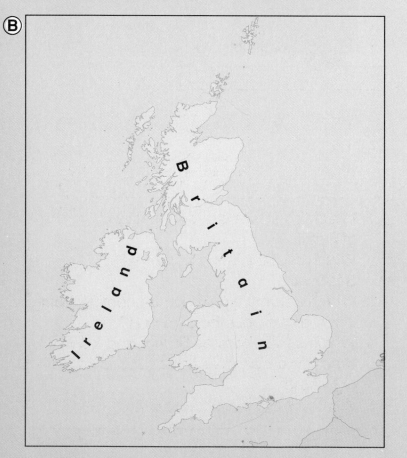

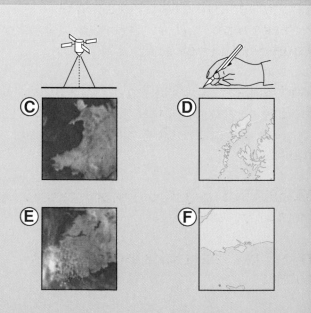

Countries of the British Isles

a map of the British Isles.
e British Isles there are five countries.
countries have been named in **G**.
will see a sign like **H** when you drive from
country into another.

and, Wales, Scotland and Northern
nd are countries in the United Kingdom.
capital city of the United Kingdom
ndon.

Republic of Ireland is a separate country.
in is its capital city.

nap **G** the seas round the British Isles
named.

Ⓗ

Croeso i Gymru
Welcome to Wales

?

1 Which countries are on the island
   of Britain?
2 Which country has a border with
   Scotland?
3 Which country would you be coming from
   if you drove past the sign in **H**?
4 Which sea separates Britain and Ireland?
5 Which two countries are on the island
   of Ireland?
6 Which seas surround the British Isles?

Looking down from space at the Earth

Photo **A** was taken from a spacecraft on its way to the Moon.
It shows one side of the Earth.
You can see that the Earth is round.
The Earth is shaped like a ball.
In photo **A** you can see where the land and sea are.
The white shapes are clouds.

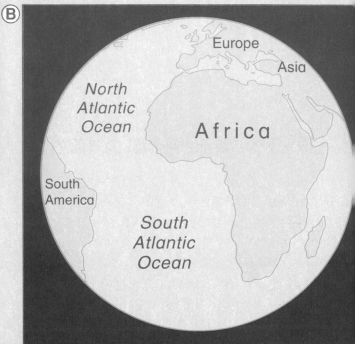

B is a map of the land and sea that you can see in **A**.
It shows the part of the Earth you can see in the space photo.
Some parts of the Earth have been named on the map.
Find Africa on the map and the space photo.

Models can be made of the Earth.
A **globe** is a model which is the shape of the Earth.
It shows land and sea.
The globe in **C** shows a view of the Earth that is different from the view in **A**.

1 Name two other parts of the Earth you can see in map **B**.
2 Draw the shape of an island you can see in map **B**.
3 Look at photo **C** of the globe. Name a part of the Earth it shows.
4 Find the British Isles in map **B**. Which part of the Earth are they in?

Continents and Oceans

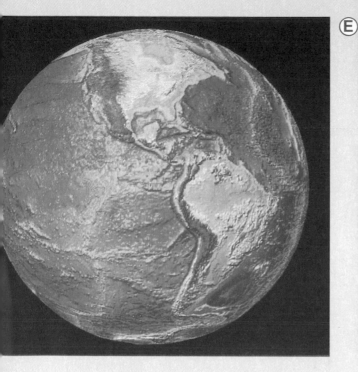

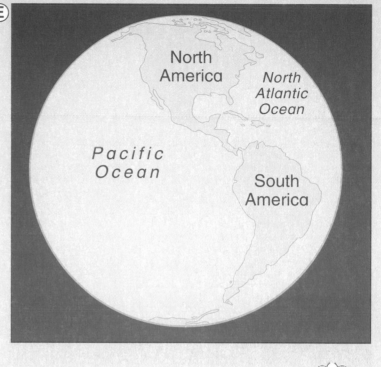

Ⓔ

to **D** shows another view of the Earth.
E names the areas of land and sea that
o **D** shows.

a map of the whole of the Earth.
ows all the areas of land and sea you can
in **B**, **C** and **E**.

large areas of land are called **continents**.
large areas of sea are called **oceans**.

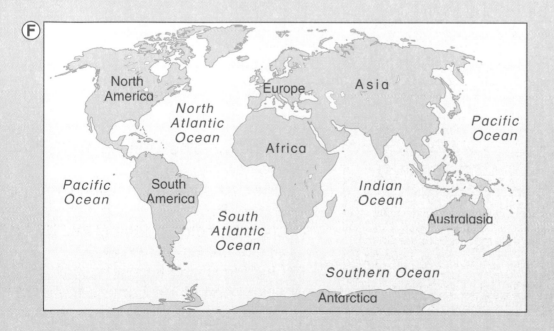

Ⓕ

?

1 Name the continents in map **F**.
2 How many continents are there?
3 Which oceans are shown in **D** and **E**?
4 Which other oceans are shown in **F**?
5 Which ocean would you cross to go from Africa to Australasia?
6 Name one continent on each side of the Pacific Ocean.

Teacher's Notes

LOOKING DOWN : PERSPECTIVE / PLAN

	Themes	Resources	Extension Activities	National Cur Links
2-3	**Representations of objects.** • oblique and vertical perspectives of ground features: how we see them • describe / record shapes of objects • develop language of perspective: shape	• gratings, hole covers, brick patterns in school grounds; floor patterns inside buildings • photos (oblique and vertical) of similar features; drawings of some	• make rubbings and drawings of floor and ground coverings in and around school and home • identify photos of features around school • identify and draw larger features looked down on, eg path, road	Working to assessmen opportunity • Gg AT 1 • Ma AT 4
4-5	**Draw around objects to make a plan.** • elevation and vertical views of a model home: how we usually see them • shape of features from above • idea of the plan of an object	• model furniture, toy buildings and vehicles etc • photos of toys from different angles, including from vertically above • drawings of base shapes of toys	• using model furniture, create layouts of rooms • match shape drawings to vertical photos and to furniture, vehicles, etc. • children draw round base shape of toys • make one correct and several inaccurate shape drawings of different toys; children to identify accurate drawing	Working to assessmen opportunity • Gg AT 1 • Ma AT 4
6-7	**Use pictures to identify features.** **Extract information from a pictorial map.** • identifying features in a familiar setting • idea of a map • introduction to picture map • relating map to photo of room	• photos of classroom at different angles • photos (oblique and vertical) and shape drawings of classroom furniture • picture map of classroom	• match shape drawings to vertical photos and/or furniture • draw round base shape of objects in classroom, school and home for others to identify • child to use photo or drawing to find feature in classroom or school	Working to assessmen opportunity • Gg AT 1 • Gg AT 1
8-9	**Extract information from pictorial maps.** • introduction to picture map of a local area • variety of features in a leisure park • introduction to locational language: eg right, left, in front of, middle, behind, next to	• picture maps of similar leisure and other locality-scale environments • photos of features in local park/playground • plan drawings of features in park	• discuss features and possible activities in area shown in picture map • visit to local park/playground using picture map to locate features • identify plans of features in local park/playground	Working to assessmen opportunity • Gg AT 1 • Ma AT 4
10-11	**Use photos to identify features and find out about places.** **Identify features on vertical aerial photographs.** • model as a micro-version of the real world • identifying features and relating oblique and vertical views • how a vertical view can help: no hidden features unlike an oblique view	• toy buildings, vehicles, people and animals • model-making resources e.g boxes, card, scissors, paste, paint • modelling on sand tray	• match shape drawings to vertical photos and/or furniture • draw round base shape of objects in classroom, school and home for others to identify • make one correct and several inaccurate shape drawings of different classroom features; children to identify accurate drawing • child to use photo or drawing to find feature in classroom or school	Working to assessmen opportunity • Gg At 1 • Gg At 1 • Gg At 1

LOCATION

	Themes	Resources	Extension Activities	National Cur Links
12-13	**Use photos to identify features and find out about places.** **Identify features on vertical aerial photos and match them to a map.** **Describe the location of places using maps.** • vocabulary of place and position: eg opposite, at the back of, between, across, beside, alongside, around, against	• map of the model made by the class • vertical photos of the class model • cue cards of location words/terms • cards with plans of individual features, and cards naming features, for matching together	• talk about what the map of the model shows, compared to the vertical photo and the model • say as precisely as possible where each feature is • games in which feature has to be identified only from what is close to or around it • location games in PE/movement lessons, using location vocabulary and apparatus	Working to assessmen opportunity • Gg AT 1 • Gg AT 1 • Gg AT 1 • Ma AT 4
14-15	**Use photos to identify features and find out about places.** **Identify features on vertical aerial photos.** • relating ground level photos to oblique photos • looking at shapes and plans of features	• ground level photos of own school and locality • oblique and vertical aerial photos of area around school • plans of features in school and locality • ground level, oblique and vertical photos of other localities	• use plans of features to find them in photos • children to draw plan shapes from photos for others to identify • say where features are in room, school and locality • games where feature is identified only from what is close to or around it	Working to assessmen opportunity • Gg AT 1 • Gg AT 1

KEY AND USE OF MAP

	Themes	Resources	Extension Activities	National Cur Links
16-17	**Interpret symbols using maps.** **Identify features on vertical aerial photos and match them to a map.** **Use maps to find out where features are located.** • using shape and colour to identify features • what a map key is	• vertical photo and map of the area around school • ground level photos of features in local area • plans of features in local area	• discuss what shapes / colours on map show • discuss the purpose of a key • discuss value of colour code for classifying and identifying features • on map of model or own locality create a colour code for features	Working to assessmen opportunity • Gg AT 1 • Gg AT 1 • Gg AT 1